THE STORY

OF

PALESTINE

by

Lalit Mohanty

INTRODUCTION

The history of Palestine is a complex, multifaceted tapestry of cultures, peoples, and empires that have left an indelible mark on the land that sits at the crossroads of the Middle East. This book, "A Tapestry of History: The Story of Palestine," delves into the rich and tumultuous history of Palestine, from its ancient origins to the present day. Our journey through time will explore the land's diverse peoples, their struggles, triumphs, and the ongoing quest for self-determination.

CHAPTER 1

ANCIENT ROOTS

In the ancient annals of history, the land known as Palestine stood at the crossroads of empires and civilizations, a place where cultures and peoples merged, diverged, and left their indelible marks. This chapter delves into the earliest origins of Palestine, examining the diverse inhabitants who laid the foundation for its rich history.

1.1 The Early Inhabitants

Palestine's history begins thousands of years ago when the land was home to a variety of indigenous peoples. Among the earliest inhabitants were the Canaanites, who lived in the region from the 4th millennium BCE. They were a Semitic people, and their cities and settlements dotted the landscape. The Canaanites' language, closely related to Hebrew and Phoenician, played a pivotal role in the development of the region's linguistic and cultural identity.

Another significant group that settled in Palestine were the Philistines, who arrived in the 12th century BCE, around the same time as the Israelite tribes. The Philistines originated from the Aegean world and established a series of city-states along the coastal plain. Their presence would significantly influence the culture and history of the region, with their name ultimately giving rise to the term "Palestine."

1.2 The Rise and Fall of Ancient Empires

Throughout its early history, Palestine was subject to the ebb and flow of powerful empires. The ancient Egyptians under Pharaoh Thutmose III extended their reach into Canaan in the 15th century BCE, leaving inscriptions and stelae attesting to their control over the territory. Later, the Hittites from Anatolia and the Mesopotamian empires, such as the Assyrians and Babylonians, vied for control over the land, each leaving their unique imprints.

1.3 The Israelite Kingdoms

One of the most well-known chapters in Palestine's ancient history is the emergence of the Israelite kingdoms. The Israelites, led by legendary figures like King David and King Solomon, established the United Monarchy, which united the tribes of Israel into a formidable kingdom. Under Solomon's rule, Jerusalem was transformed into a grand capital.

However, the United Monarchy would not last. After Solomon's death, the kingdom split into two, with the northern kingdom of Israel and the southern kingdom of Judah. These two entities faced internal strife and the pressure of external threats, with the northern kingdom falling to the Assyrians in 722 BCE and the southern kingdom eventually succumbing to the Babylonians in 586 BCE.

The Babylonian Exile that followed marked a pivotal moment in the history of the Israelites. It was during this period that the Hebrew Bible (Old Testament) began to take its final form, and the concept of monotheism, central to the Jewish faith, crystallized.

The ancient roots of Palestine, characterized by the coexistence of various cultures and the rise and fall of empires, laid the groundwork for the dynamic and diverse history that would follow. In the chapters to come, we will explore how the land continued to evolve, shaped by the influences of successive civilizations and peoples who called it home.

CHAPTER 2

ROMAN RULE AND THE BIRTH OF CHRISTIANITY

The transition from ancient empires to the dawn of a new era marked by the birth of Christianity was a transformative period in the history of Palestine. In this chapter, we explore the influence of Roman rule and the emergence of Christianity in the Holy Land.

2.1 Roman Conquest and the Era of Pax Romana

In 63 BCE, Pompey the Great of Rome invaded the region known as Judea, incorporating it into the expanding Roman Republic. This marked the beginning of Roman rule in Palestine, which would last for several centuries. Under Roman administration, the region witnessed relative stability and prosperity, as it became part of the vast Roman Empire.

The era of Roman rule brought significant changes to the landscape. Herod the Great, a client king of Rome, undertook ambitious building projects, including the reconstruction of the Second Temple in Jerusalem. The city's grandeur was further enhanced, and it became a bustling center of trade and religion.

2.2 The Life and Teachings of Jesus of Nazareth

During this period, in the first century CE, a significant religious figure emerged in the region. Jesus of Nazareth, a Jewish preacher and healer, is believed by Christians to be the Son of God and the founder of Christianity. His teachings focused on love, forgiveness, and salvation, and they challenged the religious and political authorities of his time.

Jesus' life and crucifixion in Jerusalem, as described in the New Testament, laid the groundwork for the Christian faith. His followers spread his message, and Christianity began to take root in the land that was at the heart of its sacred history.

2.3 The Growth of Christianity and the Holy Land

Christianity expanded rapidly in the centuries following the death of Jesus. The apostles and early disciples played a crucial role in disseminating the Christian message throughout the Roman Empire. The Holy Land, with Jerusalem as its spiritual center, became a destination for pilgrims and an important hub for the nascent Christian community.

The spread of Christianity in Palestine was not without challenges. It faced intermittent persecution from Roman authorities, who viewed it as a threat to the social and political order. Nevertheless, the faith persevered and grew in numbers.

In the 4th century CE, Emperor Constantine I converted to Christianity and issued the Edict of Milan, which granted religious tolerance to Christians. This marked a turning point, as Christianity went from being a persecuted minority to the official religion of the Roman Empire.

As a result, the Holy Land saw a surge in Christian pilgrims and the construction of important religious sites, such as the Church of the Holy Sepulchre, believed to be the site of Jesus' crucifixion and burial. These developments further solidified the connection between Christianity and the Holy Land, making it a central pilgrimage destination for Christians worldwide.

The influence of Roman rule and the birth of Christianity had a profound and lasting impact on the history of Palestine. As we continue our journey through time, we will explore how the region's religious and cultural diversity continued to evolve, shaped by the dynamic forces of history.

CHAPTER 3

BYZANTINE AND ISLAMIC ERAS

The transition from Roman rule to the Byzantine and Islamic periods marked a significant turning point in the history of Palestine. In this chapter, we delve into the dynamics of these two successive eras, exploring the influence of the Byzantine Empire and the dawn of Islam in the Holy Land.

3.1 The Byzantine Rule: The Spread of Christianity

With the division of the Roman Empire in 285 CE, the Eastern Roman Empire, commonly known as the Byzantine Empire, emerged as a dominant force in the region. The Byzantines continued to uphold Christianity as a central aspect of their identity and governance, reinforcing the Holy Land's significance in Christian tradition.

During the Byzantine era, Jerusalem remained a focal point for Christians. Pilgrims flocked to the city, and numerous churches and monasteries were constructed. The Church of the Nativity in Bethlehem, commemorating the birth of Jesus, and the Church of the Holy Sepulchre in Jerusalem, believed to house the crucifixion and burial sites, were among the most renowned.

The Byzantines also left a cultural imprint on Palestine through their mosaics and art. These artistic expressions depicted religious themes, biblical narratives, and the daily life of the time.

3.2 The Islamic Conquest and the Umayyad Caliphate

In the early 7th century CE, a new and transformative force swept through the region as Islam emerged. Led by the Prophet Muhammad, the Islamic community expanded rapidly. After Muhammad's death in 632 CE, his followers, known as Muslims, embarked on a series of conquests, with Palestine coming under Islamic rule.

The Islamic era brought significant changes to the Holy Land. Jerusalem, known in Arabic as Al-Quds, became a place of religious importance for Muslims. According to Islamic tradition, the Prophet Muhammad's Night Journey (Isra and Mi'raj) took him to Jerusalem before ascending to the heavens. The Dome of the Rock, built on the Temple Mount in Jerusalem, is one of the most iconic structures, symbolizing the significance of the city in Islam.

The Umayyad Caliphate, which succeeded the initial Islamic conquest, established the city of Ramla as a regional capital. The Umayyads constructed the White Mosque in the city, showcasing their architectural and artistic prowess. The Dome of the Chain and the Al-Aqsa Mosque were added to the Temple Mount in Jerusalem, further solidifying its status as a holy site.

The coexistence of Christian, Jewish, and Muslim communities during this period contributed to a rich tapestry of religious and cultural exchange. Scholars, philosophers, and theologians from various backgrounds converged, leading to intellectual and scientific advancements.

The Byzantine and Islamic eras in Palestine marked a period of religious and cultural growth, with the Holy Land becoming a focal point for multiple faiths. The influences of both empires and the emergence of Islam laid the foundation for the region's dynamic and diverse history in the centuries to come.

CHAPTER 4

CRUSADERS AND THE MEDIEVAL PERIOD

The medieval era in Palestine was marked by a series of dramatic events, with the arrival of the Crusaders being a significant turning point. In this chapter, we explore the Crusader period and its impact on the Holy Land, as well as the broader medieval dynamics that shaped Palestine.

4.1 The First Crusade and the Establishment of Crusader States

In the late 11th century, the call for a holy war to reclaim Jerusalem and the Holy Land from Muslim control spread across Europe. Pope Urban II's declaration in 1095 ignited the First Crusade. The Crusaders, comprising knights, soldiers, and religious pilgrims, embarked on a perilous journey to the East.

In 1099, after a long and arduous campaign, the Crusaders captured Jerusalem. The city, soaked in bloodshed, was handed over to the Christian forces. This marked the establishment of the Crusader States in the Levant, including the Kingdom of Jerusalem, the Principality of Antioch, the County of Tripoli, and the County of Edessa.

Jerusalem became the capital of the Kingdom of Jerusalem, and the Crusaders undertook extensive construction, fortifications, and religious projects. The Church of the Holy Sepulchre was repaired, and new Christian institutions were founded, while the Dome of the Rock was converted into a church.

4.2 The Mamluks and the Reconquest of Palestine

The Crusader States faced constant threats from Muslim forces, particularly the Ayyubids, a Kurdish dynasty established by Saladin. Saladin, famous for his military campaigns, recaptured Jerusalem in 1187, ending the Latin Christian rule in the city. The Crusaders' hold over other territories in the Levant gradually eroded.

The subsequent Mamluk Sultanate, founded by former slave soldiers, consolidated its power in Egypt and Syria and pursued a relentless campaign to retake the remaining Crusader strongholds. The Mamluks' conquest of Acre in 1291 marked the end of the Crusader presence in the Holy Land. The Crusader States were no more, and their legacy was etched into the historical memory of the region.

4.3 Ottoman Rule and the Age of Empires

Following the Mamluk era, the Ottoman Empire emerged as the dominant power in the region. Ottoman rule began in 1516 when they defeated the Mamluks at the Battle of Marj Dabiq, bringing Palestine under their control. For the next four centuries, Palestine was part of the vast Ottoman Empire.

Ottoman rule introduced a period of relative stability and prosperity to the region. The Ottomans instituted various reforms and established a system of governance that had a lasting impact on the land and its people.

The arrival of European powers in the late 19th century, along with the emergence of the Zionist movement, set the stage for significant changes in the 20th century. These events would reshape the history of Palestine and set the course for the modern era.

The medieval period in Palestine was marked by the ebb and flow of power, as different empires and forces vied for control over the Holy Land. The legacy of the Crusaders, the rise of the Mamluks, and the enduring Ottoman rule left a lasting imprint on the land and its cultural heritage. The following chapters will delve into the modern transformations that would shape the destiny of Palestine in the 20th and 21st centuries.

CHAPTER 5

MODERN TRANSFORMATIONS

The modern period in the history of Palestine witnessed a series of transformative events that reshaped the region's political, social, and cultural landscape. This chapter explores the rise of Zionism, the impact of World War I, and the subsequent changes in the 20th century that paved the way for the Israeli-Palestinian conflict.

5.1 The Rise of Zionism and Jewish Immigration

The late 19th century saw the emergence of the Zionist movement, a political and ideological movement advocating for the establishment of a Jewish homeland in Palestine. Inspired by a desire to escape anti-Semitic persecution in Europe and driven by a deep attachment to biblical and historical ties to the land, Zionist pioneers began settling in Palestine.

Zionist settlement led to tensions with the local Arab population, who resented the influx of Jewish immigrants and the Zionist vision of a Jewish state. These tensions would later become a central issue in the Israeli-Palestinian conflict.

5.2 World War I and the British Mandate

The collapse of the Ottoman Empire at the end of World War I brought about significant changes in the Middle East. In 1917, the British government issued the Balfour Declaration, expressing support for the establishment of a "national home for the Jewish people" in Palestine. The declaration ignited further tensions between the Jewish and Arab communities.

After the war, the League of Nations granted Britain the mandate to govern Palestine, and the British Mandate for Palestine was established. During this time, the Jewish population continued to grow, and Jewish-Arab tensions escalated, leading to sporadic violence and conflicts.

5.3 The Palestinian Arab Uprising and the Great Arab Revolt

In the late 1930s, a series of Palestinian Arab uprisings against British rule and Jewish immigration took place. The Arab Revolt of 1936-1939 sought to challenge British policies and halt Jewish immigration. The British Mandate authorities suppressed the revolt, but the underlying tensions between Arabs, Jews, and the British persisted.

As World War II engulfed the world, the situation in Palestine remained complex, with the international community divided on how to address the ongoing conflicts and rival claims to the land.

The modern transformations in Palestine laid the groundwork for the Israeli-Palestinian conflict, a complex and deeply rooted issue that continues to shape the region's history and politics. In the chapters that follow, we will delve into the post-World War II period, the creation of Israel, and the ongoing struggle for self-determination and peace in the Holy Land.

CHAPTER 6

THE CREATION OF ISRAEL

The establishment of the State of Israel in 1948 marked a profound turning point in the history of Palestine. This chapter explores the factors that led to the creation of Israel, the events surrounding it, and the enduring consequences of this pivotal moment.

6.1 The United Nations Partition Plan

In the aftermath of World War II and the Holocaust, the issue of Jewish refugees and the quest for a Jewish homeland became more pressing. The United Nations, founded in 1945, took on the task of addressing the Palestine question. In 1947, the UN proposed the United Nations Partition Plan for Palestine, which recommended the division of Palestine into separate Jewish and Arab states, with Jerusalem under international administration.

The partition plan was adopted by the UN General Assembly in November 1947, with strong support from Western nations, but it was vehemently opposed by Arab states and

Palestinian Arabs. The plan's implementation was to begin in 1948.

6.2 The 1948 Arab-Israeli War and Palestinian Displacement

The adoption of the partition plan led to immediate conflict. On May 14, 1948, David Ben-Gurion, head of the Jewish Agency, proclaimed the establishment of the State of Israel. This declaration was met with armed opposition from surrounding Arab states and Palestinian Arab militias.

The 1948 Arab-Israeli War, also known as the War of Independence or Nakba (Catastrophe), resulted in significant territorial changes. Israel expanded beyond the boundaries defined by the partition plan, while neighboring Arab states controlled other areas. During the war, hundreds of thousands of Palestinian Arabs were displaced from their homes, leading to a refugee crisis that persists to this day.

6.3 The Armistice Agreements and the Status of Jerusalem

In 1949, a series of armistice agreements were reached between Israel and neighboring Arab states, formally ending the 1948 war. However, these agreements did not lead to a comprehensive peace settlement, and the issue of Palestinian refugees remained unresolved.

Jerusalem, which had been designated as an international city under the UN partition plan, was divided between Israel and Jordan, with Israel controlling the western part and Jordan the eastern part. This division of Jerusalem contributed to ongoing tensions in the region.

The creation of Israel was celebrated by Jews worldwide as the realization of a long-held dream. However, it also resulted in the displacement and suffering of many Palestinian Arabs, leading to a deep-seated Palestinian refugee issue and a lasting conflict between Israelis and Palestinians.

The establishment of Israel set the stage for decades of geopolitical, social, and military conflicts in the region. In the chapters that follow, we will delve into the various aspects of the Israeli-Palestinian conflict, the struggle for statehood and self-determination, and the efforts to find a peaceful resolution to the complex and enduring challenges that continue to shape the history of Palestine.

CHAPTER 7

SIX-DAY WAR AND BEYOND

The Six-Day War of 1967 and its aftermath marked a significant turning point in the Israeli-Palestinian conflict and the history of the Middle East. This chapter explores the events leading up to the war, its outcomes, and the enduring consequences that continue to shape the region.

7.1 Background to the Six-Day War

Tensions had been building in the Middle East for years leading up to the Six-Day War. Several key factors contributed to the outbreak of hostilities:

- Border Disputes: Israel and its Arab neighbors, particularly Egypt and Syria, had ongoing disputes over border territories, including the Gaza Strip and the Golan Heights.

- Blockades and Blockades: Arab states, under Egyptian President Gamal Abdel Nasser, blockaded the Straits of Tiran, cutting off Israel's access to the Red Sea. Israel viewed this as an act of war.

- Nationalism and Ideology: Nationalism and the desire to regain territory lost in the 1948 Arab-Israeli War were strong driving forces for both sides.

7.2 The Six-Day War Unfolds

On June 5, 1967, Israel launched a preemptive strike on Egyptian airfields, swiftly incapacitating the Egyptian Air Force. This move was part of a coordinated operation with simultaneous attacks on Egyptian, Jordanian, and Syrian forces. In just six days, Israel captured the Gaza Strip and the Sinai Peninsula from Egypt, the West Bank and East Jerusalem from Jordan, and the Golan Heights from Syria.

The rapid and decisive Israeli victory reshaped the map of the Middle East. Israel now controlled significantly more territory, including the entire city of Jerusalem. The war also resulted in the displacement of Palestinian Arabs in the newly occupied territories.

7.3 Occupation and Settlements

In the aftermath of the Six-Day War, Israel began to establish settlements in the newly occupied territories. These settlements became a focal point of tension in the Israeli-Palestinian conflict. Israel's policy of building and expanding settlements in the West Bank and Gaza Strip created significant obstacles to peace negotiations and intensified the conflict.

7.4 The Yom Kippur War and Peace Efforts

In 1973, Egypt and Syria launched a surprise attack on Israel, known as the Yom Kippur War. While Israel eventually repelled the attack, the war led to a shift in the region. The war underscored the need for peace negotiations, leading to the Camp David Accords in 1978 between Israel and Egypt, resulting in the return of the Sinai Peninsula to Egyptian control.

7.5 Ongoing Conflict and Peace Initiatives

The Israeli-Palestinian conflict continued to be marked by violence, negotiations, and attempts at peace in the following decades. The Oslo Accords of the 1990s laid the groundwork for Palestinian self-governance, but peace efforts remained elusive. The construction of the Israeli West Bank barrier and ongoing clashes in Gaza further complicated the situation.

Efforts by international actors and leaders to broker a lasting peace between Israelis and Palestinians persist, but the conflict remains unresolved, with its root causes deeply entrenched in historical grievances, territorial disputes, and questions of identity and self-determination.

The Six-Day War and its aftermath have left an indelible mark on the history of the Middle East. The continued struggle for peace in the region, the status of Jerusalem, the plight of Palestinian refugees, and the complex issues of borders and territory are among the enduring challenges that shape the ongoing history of Palestine and the broader Middle East.

CHAPTER 8

THE CONTEMPORARY STRUGGLE

The contemporary struggle in Palestine is marked by ongoing conflicts, peace efforts, and the pursuit of self-determination. This chapter delves into the events and developments that have defined the region's recent history, including intifadas, peace negotiations, and the broader context of the Israeli-Palestinian conflict.

8.1 Intifadas and Violence in the Late 20th Century

The late 20th century witnessed two major Palestinian uprisings, known as intifadas, against Israeli occupation:

- The First Intifada (1987-1993): This largely nonviolent uprising saw Palestinians engage in acts of civil disobedience, protests, and strikes against Israeli rule. The intifada had a profound impact on the

Israeli-Palestinian conflict and led to the Oslo Accords.

- The Second Intifada (2000-2005): Marked by violence and suicide bombings, this uprising followed the breakdown of the Camp David talks and escalated tensions. The conflict resulted in significant loss of life on both sides and led to the construction of the Israeli West Bank barrier.

8.2 The Oslo Accords and the Path to Palestinian Autonomy

In the early 1990s, the Oslo Accords represented a breakthrough in Israeli-Palestinian relations. Negotiated in secret talks, the accords led to the creation of the Palestinian Authority (PA), an interim self-governing body in parts of the West Bank and Gaza Strip. Yasser Arafat became the PA's first president.

Despite the hopes for a peaceful resolution, the peace process encountered significant obstacles and periods of breakdown, including the assassination of Israeli Prime Minister Yitzhak Rabin in 1995 and continued violence.

8.3 The Barrier Wall and the Gaza Strip

In the wake of the Second Intifada, Israel began constructing a barrier wall, primarily in the West Bank. Israel cited security concerns for its construction, while Palestinians saw it as a land-grab and a further obstacle to the creation of a viable Palestinian state.

The Gaza Strip, controlled by Hamas after elections in 2006, experienced numerous conflicts with Israel, including the 2008-2009 Gaza War, the 2012 conflict, and the 2014 Gaza War. The situation in Gaza remains dire, with a blockade that severely limits the movement of goods and people, contributing to humanitarian challenges.

8.4 Diplomatic Efforts and Peace Process

Throughout the contemporary struggle, numerous diplomatic efforts have been made to find a peaceful resolution to the Israeli-Palestinian conflict. These include the Road Map for Peace, the Annapolis Conference, and the efforts of various mediators and international actors.

However, the challenges of borders, the status of Jerusalem, the fate of Palestinian refugees, and the issue of Israeli settlements in the West Bank continue to be central points of contention. Despite the persistent efforts of leaders and diplomats, a comprehensive peace agreement remains elusive.

The contemporary struggle in Palestine is characterized by ongoing tensions, periods of violence, and attempts to navigate a complex and deeply rooted conflict. The search for a just and lasting solution continues, with the history of the region continually evolving as new developments and challenges shape the future of Palestine and its quest for self-determination.

CHAPTER 9

PRESENT CHALLENGES AND
FUTURE PROSPECTS

The present challenges and future prospects in Palestine are deeply intertwined with the complex and protracted Israeli-Palestinian conflict. This chapter explores the current state of affairs, the ongoing issues facing the region, and potential paths forward.

9.1 Contemporary Challenges

The Israeli-Palestinian conflict remains at the heart of the challenges facing Palestine. Several key issues continue to impact the region:

- **Settlements:** Israeli settlements in the West Bank and East Jerusalem remain a contentious issue, complicating the prospects for a two-state solution.

These settlements have expanded over the years, making the delineation of borders more complex.

- **Gaza Blockade:** The blockade of the Gaza Strip by Israel has created a humanitarian crisis. The severe restrictions on the movement of goods and people have led to economic hardship and limited access to essential services.

- **Status of Jerusalem:** The status of Jerusalem, a city claimed as the capital by both Israelis and Palestinians, remains a contentious issue. Its final status is a key point of negotiation.

- **Refugees:** The question of Palestinian refugees, both those displaced in 1948 and their descendants, is a deeply sensitive issue with implications for any potential peace settlement.

- **Security Concerns:** Israel cites security concerns as a central factor in its policies, including the construction of the West Bank barrier and restrictions on movement.

9.2 Political Divisions

Internal divisions among Palestinians have further complicated efforts to address the broader challenges. The division between the Fatah-dominated Palestinian Authority in the West Bank and Hamas in the Gaza Strip has hindered Palestinian unity and weakened their negotiating position.

9.3 International Involvement

International actors, including the United Nations, the United States, the European Union, and Arab states, have been involved in mediating the Israeli-Palestinian conflict. However, efforts to broker a comprehensive peace agreement have faced significant hurdles.

9.4 Future Prospects

The prospects for a resolution to the Israeli-Palestinian conflict remain uncertain, with a range of possible outcomes:

- **Two-State Solution:** The idea of a two-state solution, with Israel and a Palestinian state living side by side in peace, has been a longstanding goal of international diplomacy. However, challenges such as settlements and political divisions continue to hinder progress.

- **One-State Solution:** Some have proposed a one-state solution in which Israelis and Palestinians share a single, democratic state. However, this idea faces significant opposition and complex questions about power-sharing and minority rights.

- **Continued Conflict:** The status quo of continued conflict and periodic violence is another possible outcome, with ongoing tensions and territorial disputes.

- **Renewed Diplomacy:** Diplomatic efforts continue, and future negotiations could potentially yield a breakthrough. International actors and regional dynamics will play a crucial role in shaping the course of future negotiations.

- **Humanitarian and Economic Development:** Improved living conditions, economic development, and international aid efforts can provide much-needed relief and opportunities for Palestinians. Initiatives aimed at enhancing the well-being and prospects of the Palestinian people are essential.

The challenges and future prospects in Palestine are marked by uncertainty, complexity, and deep-rooted historical grievances. The path forward will depend on the efforts of leaders, international actors, and the aspirations of Israelis and Palestinians for a just and lasting resolution to the Israeli-Palestinian conflict, along with a peaceful and prosperous future for the region.

CHAPTER 10

THE PEOPLE OF PALESTINE

The story of Palestine is not just one of political conflict; it's also the narrative of a diverse and resilient population with a rich cultural heritage. In this chapter, we delve into the unique identity and experiences of the people of Palestine.

10.1 Diverse Ethnic and Religious Composition

Palestine's population is characterized by its diverse ethnic and religious makeup. The majority of Palestinians are Arab, primarily of Palestinian Arab descent, but there are also minority groups, including Bedouins, Circassians, and Armenians. This diversity is reflective of the historical and cultural exchanges that have taken place in the region.

Religiously, the majority of Palestinians are Muslim, with a significant Christian minority, particularly in Bethlehem,

Jerusalem, and other historic Christian centers. Religious diversity is a defining feature of the region, with people of different faiths coexisting and sharing historical and cultural ties.

10.2 Cultural Heritage and Identity

Palestinians take great pride in their cultural heritage and national identity. This identity is rooted in a long history of civilization, influenced by Canaanite, Philistine, Hebrew, Assyrian, Babylonian, Roman, and Arab cultures. Palestinians maintain their unique traditions, including cuisine, music, dance, and dress. The rich tapestry of Palestinian heritage is a source of cultural strength and resilience.

10.3 Resilience and Creativity

The Palestinian people have shown remarkable resilience in the face of adversity. Despite the challenges posed by conflict and occupation, Palestinians have preserved their cultural traditions, maintained a strong sense of identity, and demonstrated an indomitable spirit. Art, literature, and music have played a significant role in conveying their experiences and aspirations to the world.

10.4 The Voices of Palestinians

It's essential to listen to the voices of Palestinians themselves. Many Palestinians share a common aspiration for self-determination and statehood, as well as a desire for peace and justice. Yet, there are diverse opinions within the

Palestinian community about the path forward, the strategies for achieving their goals, and the nature of future relations with Israel.

The diaspora community of Palestinian refugees, who were displaced during various conflicts, also plays a critical role in preserving Palestinian identity and advocating for their rights. Palestinian communities exist worldwide, with large populations in neighboring Arab countries and the global Palestinian diaspora.

10.5 The Challenges and Hopes of the Future

The future of the Palestinian people remains intertwined with the quest for a peaceful resolution to the Israeli-Palestinian conflict. Many Palestinians hope for a sovereign state of their own and the right to determine their own destiny. However, they continue to face complex challenges, including political divisions, economic hardships, and the impact of the ongoing conflict on their daily lives.

The people of Palestine have shown extraordinary strength and resilience in the face of historical injustices and ongoing challenges. Their cultural heritage, identity, and unwavering hope for a brighter future are integral components of the Palestinian story. As the search for a just and lasting resolution to the Israeli-Palestinian conflict continues, the voices and experiences of the Palestinian people will remain central to the narrative of Palestine's history and its potential for peace and prosperity.

CONCLUSION

The history of Palestine is a tale of enduring struggle, tenacity, and the quest for self-determination. "A Tapestry of History: The Story of Palestine" takes readers on a captivating journey through the centuries, shedding light on the multifaceted dynamics of this land and its people. As the world continues to grapple with the challenges of the Israeli-Palestinian conflict, this book serves as a testament to the importance of understanding the historical context that has shaped the region. It is our hope that a deeper understanding of this history can contribute to a more peaceful and just future for all those who call Palestine home.

APPENDIX

KEY DATES AND TERMS

This appendix provides a concise reference for key historical dates, events, and terms related to the history of Palestine. These are central to understanding the complex narrative of the region.

A.1 Key Historical Dates:

- **4th millennium BCE:** Canaanites inhabit the region.

- **12th century BCE:** Philistines arrive in Palestine.

- **6th century BCE:** Babylonian Exile.

- **1st century CE:** Birth of Jesus of Nazareth.

- **4th century CE:** Roman rule over Palestine.

- **7th century CE:** Islamic conquest of Palestine.

- **11th-13th centuries:** Crusader states in the Holy Land.

- **16th century:** Ottoman rule over Palestine.

- **20th century:** Zionist movement and British Mandate.

- **1948:** Creation of the State of Israel.

- **1967:** Six-Day War.

- **1987-1993:** First Intifada.

- **2000-2005:** Second Intifada.

- **1993:** Oslo Accords.

- **2005-present:** Gaza blockade.

A.2 Key Terms:

- **Zionism:** A political and ideological movement advocating for the establishment of a Jewish homeland in Palestine.

- **Nakba:** "Catastrophe" in Arabic, referring to the Palestinian exodus in 1948.

- **Intifada:** Arabic for "uprising," used to describe Palestinian protests and resistance.

- **Palestinian Authority (PA):** An interim self-governing body in parts of the West Bank and Gaza Strip.

- **Two-State Solution:** A proposed resolution to the Israeli-Palestinian conflict, envisioning two states living side by side in peace.

- **One-State Solution:** Proposal for a single, democratic state for Israelis and Palestinians.

- **Gaza Strip:** A Palestinian territory controlled by Hamas.

- **West Bank:** A Palestinian territory with a complex political status due to Israeli settlements.

- **Jerusalem:** A city claimed as a capital by both Israelis and Palestinians, with international significance.

- **Refugees:** Palestinians displaced from their homes during conflicts in 1948 and their descendants.

- **Israeli Settlements:** Jewish communities in the West Bank and East Jerusalem, considered illegal by international law.

ABOUT THE AUTHOR

Lalit Prasad Mohanty

Contact [+917852957053]

Mr. Mohanty holds a Master of Science (MSc) degree in Mathematics, which he acquired through rigorous study and a relentless pursuit of mathematical knowledge. His deep understanding of mathematical concepts, theories, and applications has made him an authority in the field, with a reputation for clarity and an ability to convey complex ideas in an accessible manner.

In addition to his mathematical expertise, Mr. Mohanty is a dedicated educator with a Bachelor of Education (B.Ed) degree. His passion for teaching and sharing knowledge has shaped the minds of countless students, making him a respected figure in the educational community. His ability to communicate abstract concepts in a way that resonates with learners is a testament to his pedagogical skills.

Beyond his academic and professional achievements, Mr. Mohanty's foray into the history of Palestine demonstrates his intellectual curiosity and his commitment to understanding complex global issues. His book, which explores the history of Palestine, showcases his versatility as an author, as he navigates between the worlds of mathematics and history, connecting seemingly disparate disciplines in a compelling and insightful manner.

As an author, educator, and mathematician, Lalit Prasad Mohanty brings a wealth of knowledge, a passion for learning, and an interdisciplinary perspective to his work. His exploration of the history of Palestine is a testament to his intellectual curiosity and his dedication to expanding his horizons. Whether teaching the next generation of mathematicians or delving into historical narratives, Mr. Mohanty's commitment to education and knowledge dissemination is at the heart of his endeavors.

Printed in Great Britain
by Amazon

36316457R00030